Discovering

BIRDS OF PREY

M. J. Thomas and E. Soothill

The Bookwright Press
New York · 1986

Discovering Nature

Discovering Ants
Discovering Bees and Wasps
Discovering Birds of Prey
Discovering Butterflies and Moths
Discovering Frogs and Toads
Discovering Rabbits and Hares
Discovering Snakes and Lizards
Discovering Spiders
Discovering Worms

Further titles are in preparation

First published in the United States in 1986 by
The Bookwright Press
387 Park Avenue South
New York, NY 10016

First published in 1985 by
Wayland (Publishers) Limited
61 Western Road, Hove
East Sussex, BN3 1JD, England

ISBN 0-531-18052-2

Library of Congress Catalog Card Number: 85-73588
Typeset by Planagraphic Typesetters Limited
Printed in Italy by G. Canale & C.S.p.A., Turin

Contents

Introducing Birds of Prey

What is a Bird of Prey?

Any bird that eats other animals ought to be called a bird of prey. If this were so, almost every bird would be included, even a tiny wren feeding on a caterpillar, or a blackbird eating a worm. Few birds are true plant-eaters. Although finches eat mainly seeds, they will often feed their chicks on insects.

But the real birds of prey are those that have very strong, hooked beaks and powerful **taloned** feet. These are vital tools for killing and tearing up **prey.**

Birds of prey are divided into two groups. Owls make up one group. There are 133 different kinds of owls in the world. Most owls hunt at night and are called nocturnal hunters. But a few can be

A hawk owl perched on a branch keeps a lookout for something to eat.

seen hunting in daylight. The hawk owl, for instance, does most of its hunting during the morning and evening.

In the other group of birds of prey, there are the vultures, eagles, hawks, kites and falcons. All the birds in this group tend to hunt during the day and are called diurnal hunters. There are 287 different types of birds in this group.

Birds of prey are found all over the world, except in Antarctica. Only a few kinds are **cosmopolitan**, the fish-eating osprey and the peregrine falcon.

Some birds of prey are found in only one or two places. The Forster's caracara, for example, is found in the wild only on the Falkland and Cape Horn Islands. These are groups of quite small islands, near the tip of South America. By looking at a map of the world you will see just how small they are.

Right *Australia is the home of the wedge-tailed eagle but they can be found in some zoos.*

Looking at Birds of Prey

Birds of prey are much more powerful than other birds of the same size. The largest of them all is the Andean condor from South America. It has a wingspan of over 3 meters (10 feet) and weighs up to 11 kilos (24 pounds). The harpy eagle is not as big as a condor but it is probably the strongest bird in the world.

Other birds of prey, such as some owls, are tiny. The saw-whet owl is not much bigger than a house sparrow.

The eyes of birds of prey are nearer the front of the head than those of other birds. This gives them a special type of vision, called binocular vision. They can judge distances well. This special eyesight is essential for hunting prey.

Birds like condors and vultures, which eat large animals, have the biggest and most powerful beaks. On the other hand,

One of the smallest kinds of owl is the saw-whet owl.

10

Above *An Andean condor in flight.*

Below *A sharp-shinned hawk.*

birds such as the sparrowhawk, which feed mainly on other small birds, manage quite well with a short beak.

Apart from having good eyesight, birds of prey must be able to hear well too. A small animal moving around on the floor of a dense forest cannot always be seen. So a bird of prey, perched above the ground, relies on sound to locate its prey.

Owls, which mainly hunt at night, have superb hearing. Their ears are on either side of the head and are hidden by feathers. They are not on top of the head as might be expected when looking at an eagle owl, for example. What look like ears are really just tufts of feathers.

The body of a bird of prey is small compared to the area of its wings.

Below *The tufts of feathers on top of an eagle owl's head are for display.*

Above *The eagle owl has strong legs, and sharp talons for gripping its prey.*

Vultures and eagles rely on their long wingspan to soar high in the sky. Warm air currents called thermals rise up from the ground and give them lift. Soaring birds rarely need to flap their wings.

Hawks and falcons must be able to put on a sudden burst of speed when hunting. Their wings are smaller and narrower and the bird can flap them easily in order to gain speed.

Kestrels are often seen hovering above

black vulture

peregrine falcon

open country. They need to flap their wings vigorously to stay over the same patch of land, where they might have seen a mouse on the ground.

Tails are very important. They are used mainly for steering, especially in confined spaces. Just imagine how difficult it must be to chase a small bird through a dense forest. The African long-tailed hawk is well adapted for this. It uses its long, fan-shaped tail to steer between the trees. The tail is also used for braking.

A bird of prey's feet are special too. Most birds of prey have neddle-sharp

The picture above shows a black vulture and a peregrine falcon. You can see the difference in size of their wings.

talons or claws, vital for killing prey. The harpy eagle has huge, powerful legs and feet for seizing and killing animals. The sparrowhawk has long legs and slender toes for catching small birds.

Fish are very slippery, but the osprey has really strong toes for gripping them tightly. Most vultures feed on dead animals. Since they do not kill, their feet are more like those of hens.

13

Where Birds of Prey Live

Several birds of prey prefer one type of **habitat** only. In Europe and North America, woodlands are a familiar habitat. Birds such as the common buzzard can be found in both **coniferous** and **deciduous** woods. The goshawk and sparrowhawk prefer woodlands too. It is probably because food is plentiful there. Both will eat other birds, up to the size of a pigeon. Woods also offer them a lot of possible nesting sites.

Some of these birds are seen quite often. But this is not true of the birds of prey living deep inside the jungle of the tropical forests. This is where the world's most fearsome birds live. They are the huge harpy eagle of South America and the Philippine monkey-eating eagle.

A female sparrowhawk nesting in the woods.

Below *A fish eagle with a catfish.*

Birds such as the osprey, fishing buzzard, sea eagle and fish eagle need to be near water. But they eat not only fish — they also eat animals such as frogs, toads and even water birds. These birds of prey live by the seashore, near lakes and rivers, and even in marshes and reedbeds, which is where the marsh harrier can be found.

What about places where there are no

A snowy owl keeps its babies warm.

trees? The cold, treeless Arctic **tundra** is the home of the snowy owl. It manages to survive the severe weather by eating small animals such as hares and lemmings. Although the gyrfalcon is found in other places, it prefers the tundra as a habitat. It is the most powerful falcon in the world.

Some birds of prey live in the desert. Living in the tundra is harsh because of the cold, but surviving in the desert can be just as tough. During the day, the heat is overpowering. Prey, such as lizards and snakes, seek shelter and only come out when the sun has gone down. This means that the birds of prey have to hunt very early in the morning or during that night.

Although quite common in other habitats, the golden eagle is also found in the northern Sahara desert, and the red-tailed hawk nests in the Arizona desert. They seem to be able to find enough food and water to survive.

Between areas of desert and tropical forest, lies the richest habitat of all. This is the tropical savanna. It is the type of land found in much South America, Africa and Southern Asia. About 120 different kinds of birds of prey live in this habitat.

Below *A red-tailed hawk soars majestically above its desert homeland.*

Savanna is mainly grassland, which in the dry season often catches fire. A few trees and shrubs are sprinkled across the land. Large numbers of big animals live in the savanna. As a result, **carrion**-eating vultures are common.

Strangely, some birds of prey prefer to live in towns. Some vultures, and birds like the black kite, are quite happy to **scavenge** in garbage dumps. Not all of

Griffon and African white-backed vultures feeding on a dead animal on the African savanna.

them are scavengers though. Some live in towns because of the cliff-like nesting places available on buildings. Many kestrels live in towns for this reason. They can also feed on the rats and mice that exist where people live.

Food and Feeding

Hunting and Killing

Birds of prey hunt and kill in many ways. Probably the most common method is to sit on a perch and watch for any movement made by an insect or a small animal. A buzzard often perches on a post, watching the ground below for movement. Then, in a flash, it swoops down to catch its prey.

A tawny owl, with its beak full of insects, perches on a tree trunk.

In open places there are few perches to be found. Some other hunting method has to be used. Birds such as the barn owl and the hen harrier fly slowly and close to the ground. When they see suitable food, they drop down on it.

A kestrel can stay above the same patch of ground for a long time. It does this by spreading out its wings and long tail feathers. The wind gives it the lift needed to float in the air. Kestrels are often seen

Below *This barn owl has caught a rat.*

hovering above the banks beside busy roads. Such places are not disturbed by people, so lots of small mice and shrews live there.

Some birds of prey hunt in the air. They chase and catch smaller birds in flight. The peregrine falcon reaches speeds of up to 320 kilometers per hour (200 miles per hour) when it dives toward a flying bird. It is one of the most

An osprey plunges feet-first into the water to catch a fish.

spectacular hunters of all birds of prey.

The osprey can catch nine fish in ten attempts. Flying some 50 meters (164 feet) above water, it dives down into the water feet-first, with a huge splash. The fish is caught in the osprey's powerful talons and taken to a nearby perch to be eaten.

19

Types of Food

The different birds of prey eat many kinds of food, from insects to an elephant that may have died of old age. Some birds of prey have to work harder than others to find food. Think how difficult it would be to catch a flying insect. This is what the Mississippi kite does in North America, grasping the insect in one of its feet.

Other birds of prey have an easier job. In Africa, swarms of **termites** emerging from their nests are gobbled up by tawny eagles. Honey buzzards prefer to eat wasp grubs. Perching near an open space, the buzzard watches adult wasps returning to their underground nests. It then digs a

Below *A stork watches several vultures eating a dead elephant.*

deep hole to get to the grubs. The bird eats some wasps too, biting off the sting before swallowing the rest of the body.

Worms, slugs and snails are easy prey. Many of the smaller owls enjoy worms and the kestrel even skins a slug before eating it. A snail's hard shell should protect it from being eaten, but the South American snail kite has a long, thin, curved beak which it inserts into the shell

This little owl has caught a large, juicy worm.

to remove the juicy snail.

The snake eagle eats poisonous snakes, like cobras. Rough scales on the eagle's legs help to protect it from snake bites. After a hard struggle, the snake becomes tired. The eagle then crushes the dangerous head before eating the snake.

Some birds of prey eat other birds' eggs. The Indian black eagle snatches eggs from nests as it flies past. The Egyptian vulture throws pelican and flamingo eggs at rocks to break the hard shells. After eggs have hatched the young chicks are

A sharp-shinned hawk watches over its young which could easily become prey for an eagle.

also stolen for prey. Fully-grown birds are eaten too.

Many birds of prey eat only one kind of food, like the bat hawk in Africa and the crab hawk of South America. The African palm nut vulture's main food is the fruit of the oil palm, although it does eat some carrion too.

In most cases the bigger the bird, the bigger its prey. Golden eagles weigh up

These are pellets from three different kinds of owls.

to 5½ kilos (12 pounds) and kill animals such as rabbits and hares.

Large animals weighing more than 10 kilos (22 pounds) cannot usually be killed by any bird of prey. Vultures wait for an animal to die before pouncing on it. As many as one hundred vultures may feed on a zebra carcass in Africa.

A good way of finding out what a bird of prey has eaten is to look at its pellets. These contain parts that the bird cannot digest, like bones, teeth, claws, beaks, feathers, fur and insect wings. These are spit out of the bird's mouth from time to time in the form of a ball, or pellet.

Reproduction

Courting and Mating

During the **breeding season,** most birds of prey follow the same pattern of events. It is a busy time for them. At the start of the season, they tend to look their best. After all, they need to attract a mate.

Birds like "showing off" in front of their mates. These **courting displays** can be quite spectacular. For example, the male hen harrier songs high up in the air before plunging quickly downward, spinning like an airplane out of control. He manages to recover just before hitting the ground. He does this to impress the female watching nearby and may repeat the display several times.

Below *A male hen harrier performs his courtship display.*

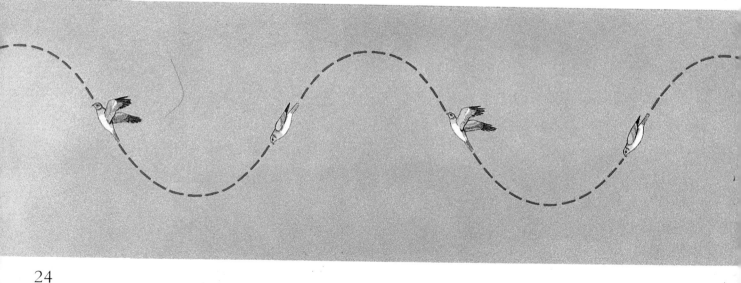

le

female

1.

2.

3.

Male and female African fish eagles perform together. In midair, they lock their claws while cartwheeling and tumbling downward.

Birds of prey call to each other too. In thick woodland this is the most common way of communicating because there is very little room for flying displays.

A pair of African fish eagles courting in midair.

Vultures have a different way of showing off. They display the bright colors on their heads and necks.

Display is soon followed by **mating** and nest building.

25

Building a Nest

Like other birds, the birds of prey build all kinds of nests in all sorts of places. Usually, the bigger the bird, the bigger the nest. Bald and golden eagles sometimes build huge nests up to 2 meters (6½ feet) wide and 5 meters (16 feet) deep. Ospreys build enormous nests of sticks. Although most nests tend to be high up in tall trees, some are built in the most unusual places.

The burrowing owl from North America nests in a hole in the ground. Its name suggests that it can dig its own hole, but in fact it prefers to take over one that has been dug by another animal. Its choice of nest material is also a bit odd — it uses dried horse manure.

Holes in trees are commonly used by birds of prey. Owls, especially, like to nest in them. Often, the hole is just large

A Swainson's hawk's nest on the roof of a wooden cabin.

enough for the owl to get in, so that the eggs and chicks are fairly safe from **predators.**

Other birds of prey, like the hen harrier and short-eared owl, nest on the ground. The nest is usually well-hidden in the undergrowth.

This bald eagle's nest, high up in a tree, is safe from predators.

Some falcons, like the peregrine, make no nest at all. The **aerie** is just a scrape in the ground, perhaps on a cliff ledge where the eggs are safe from thieves.

27

Eggs and Chicks

Birds of prey usually lay rounded oval-shaped eggs. Most lay about three eggs or fewer, but hen harriers may lay up to seven. Some owls have big **clutches** too. The long-eared owl lays as many as ten eggs in some years, especially when there is a lot of food available. It will certainly need all the food it can catch if every one of the ten eggs hatches successfully.

Eggs hatch in the normal way. The chick cuts its way out with its egg tooth, squeaking with every move. The process can take a long time, sometimes a day or

Below   *A short-eared owl's nest with several young and two eggs.*

two with the large eagle eggs. But before hatching takes place, the eggs have to be kept warm. This is called incubation. The female bird does most of the incubating, which means sitting on the eggs. Large birds of prey, like the eagles, vultures and condors, incubate for up to seven weeks. Four weeks in normal for smaller birds.

Because incubation usually starts as

A long-eared owl sits on its nest and watches over its young.

soon as the first egg is laid, the eggs hatch at different times. A whole week may pass from the time the first egg hatches to the last. This means that when the last chick breaks out, one of its brothers or sisters in the nest will be a week older.

Sad to say, only the oldest chicks tend to survive. They are stronger and bigger, which means that they are able to get to the food first when the parents bring some to the nest. Also, it is not unusual for the smallest and weakest chick to be eaten by the others.

The male bird does very little. He cannot lay eggs and rarely helps with the incubation. But he does help with the feeding of the chicks. At the beginning, the chicks are covered with soft down and are quite helpless. The adult bird has to tear off bits of meat from the prey and give small pieces to each chick.

One of the smallest kinds of falcon, a merlin, feeding its young.

Young kestrels waiting patiently to be fed.

Gradually, a few feathers begin to grow through the white down. This may happen after about ten days or so, but with the bigger birds of prey it can take several weeks. As more and more feathers grow, the beak and feet develop too. Now the young are able to feed themselves. Food is brought to the nest and left for the young to squabble over. These fights for food can be very noisy.

Altogether, baby kestrels spend about thirty days in the nest-hole. Bigger birds, such as young eagles or vultures, stay in their nests for over three months.

Migration and Other Journeys

When all or most of a particular group of birds make a long journey from one place to another at the same time every year, they are said to migrate. The birds move from their home, or breeding area, to another place where they do not breed.

The journey can be a very long one. The Swainson's hawk, for instance, breeds in Central and North America, but in the autumn all these hawks move south

Below *A family of Swainson's hawks on their nest.*

Right *In the autumn Swainson's hawks travel a long way to their winter home.*

Breeding Area

Wintering Area

Immatures' Wintering Area

The Breeding and Wintering Areas of the Swainson's Hawk

to Argentina. This is a journey of about 15,000 kilometers (9,300 miles). In the spring, they return to their breeding grounds. In one year, a Swainson's hawk may travel more than 30,000 kilometers (18,600 miles).

Why do birds migrate? The answer is a simple one. It is the need to find food.

A honey buzzard glides through the air. The feathers of its outstretched wings make a lovely pattern.

Usually, a bird of prey's food supply is less plentiful in winter. To survive, it must go to a country where it is warmer and where food is easier to find.

A honey buzzard breeding in a wood in northern Europe will have no trouble finding enough wasp grubs to eat during the summer months. But, if it stayed on until winter, it would probably starve because there would be no grubs for it to eat. So, to survive, it needs to go to a warmer country. Every year, at the end of the summer, it goes on a 10,000 kilometer (6,200 mile) trip to the southern parts of Africa. There it will find all the food it needs to survive. **Ornithologists** believe the honey buzzards do not eat at all during these long trips. Perhaps this is because much of the journey is over the Sahara Desert, where they would not find suitable food.

Some birds of prey are known as partial

Right *An adult long-eared owl stares into the camera lens.*

migrants. This is because not all of them migrate. The long-eared owl is a typical example. Some of the ones breeding in Scandinavia move southwest to warmer Britain in winter to join those already there, but others remain behind in northern Europe.

Winter in the Arctic cannot be much fun. Many of the snowy owls that nest there in summer move southward to warmer places. Snowy owls from Alaska may fly as far south as the central United States. This is because it is almost impossible to find food under a thick blanket of snow.

Most birds of prey do not migrate at all. Only about seventy types can be called migrants. The several hundred other kinds survive quite well within their breeding areas. This is because the weather and food supply remain good throughout the year.

There are other movements of birds too, but, unlike migration, they show no regular pattern. These **nomadic** movements can occur at any time and the birds can move anywhere. Usually they happen because of a change in the food supply. In a way, they can be compared to the movement of hungry people from one part of the world to another, in search of food and water.

Short-eared owls are nomads. Voles (field mice) are their favorite food, and it is quite common for vole-**plagues** to break out in some hilly areas in Europe. When this happens the short-eared owls may move quickly into the area where the field voles are plentiful.

Vultures move around in Africa too, depending on where the most carrion is to be found.

Like people, some birds of prey are just wanderers. Once, a black sparrowhawk was found on a ship off the African coast. It was hundreds of miles away from its forest home.

Short-eared owls nest on the ground. This one is incubating its eggs.

Threats and Protection

Danger of Extinction

Many birds of prey are in danger of becoming **extinct.** Humans are mainly to blame for this. Only about eighty Philippine monkey-eating eagles are left in the

A peregrin falcon with its young on a cliff nesting site.

wild. Even fewer Mauritius kestrels exist, probably no more than ten.

There are several reasons for this. Birds of prey are shot, poisoned or trapped. In some parts of Africa, they are hunted for food. Many peregrine falcons were shot during the World War II, because they ate homing pigeons, which were used for carrying important messages.

Some birds of prey are very valuable. Recently, peregrine chicks have been stolen from nests so that the thieves can sell them at a high price.

Gamekeepers blame birds of prey for taking grouse or pheasants, and sheep-farmers blame them for killing lambs. But, quite often, the bird of prey is not guilty. Often, the lamb will already be be dead before the eagle gets to it. Golden eagles have been shot in many countries.

A golden eagle with another twig for the nest it is building.

In some parts of the United States, they have even been hunted from airplanes.

Birds of prey are sometimes disturbed by people. For instance, an eagle or peregrine falcon will not put up with hikers walking past its nest too often. The bird will probably desert its nest and this means that the eggs will not hatch.

So, fewer eagles or peregrine falcons will survive. Rock climbers do not mean to harm the birds. They may be climbing a rock face, not realizing that there is a bird of prey like a gyrfalcon nesting nearby. If the climbers are there for most of the day, the gyrfalcon may leave its nest never to return.

In most countries, pesticides are a big problem. These are the chemicals farmers spray on their land to kill pests. Small birds or animals eating the pests will get a dose of poison too. Moving further along the **food chain,** if a bird of prey eats the small bird or animal, it too will be poisoned. If it eats a lot of poisoned prey, the chances are that it will die. Pesticides also cause birds to lay thin-shelled eggs, which break easily. In North America bald eagles have suffered in this way.

In many parts of the world, forests are being destroyed at an alarming rate,

This gyrfalcon and its chicks have not been disturbed by climbers.

40

because of the demand for timber. When trees are cut down, birds of prey lose their homes. This is the reason for the serious fall in the number of monkey-eating eagles and Mauritius kestrels.

A different problem exists in some countries like Britain. Large areas of moorland are being planted with conifer trees. Moorland is the habitat of the merlin. However, creating forests does have its advantages. Both the hen harrier and short-eared owl are quite at home in small conifer forests.

Below *This fierce-looking bird is a North American bald eagle.*

Below *A hen harrier on its nest.*

Protecting Birds of Prey

There are many ways to protect birds of prey. For example, the penalties against those caught killing or stealing birds of prey could be made more severe; forests, and other places where birds of prey live, could be protected; and there could be stronger controls on the dangerous chemicals used to kill pests.

Some good work is already being done. Zoos play an important part in **conservation.** Several kinds of birds of prey have been bred in captivity, like the wedge-tailed eagle. Over the years, huge numbers of wedge-tailed eagles have been destroyed in Australia because they killed sheep and lambs for food. However, a "wedge-tail" will eat a few thousand rabbits in its lifetime. This helps the farmer, because the rabbits eat the grass that his sheep feed on.

The best place to find a Forster's caracara is in a zoo.

Above *A nest box put up in a tree for kestrels or tawny owls.*

Another way to help birds of prey is to put up nest boxes for them. Kestrels will readily use a nest box. New farm buildings do not provide barn owls with as many good nesting places as the old ones did. Farmers are now being asked to put up nest boxes on their farms to encourage more barn owls to breed.

In the future, "egg-transfer" may work. Common buzzards are numerous in Britain, but red kites are scarce. The kites only nest in central Wales. To help spread red kites, perhaps eggs from their nests could be transferred to a buzzard's nest. This needs a lot of thought and planning and it must be done by experts, but some day it may work.

Below *A common buzzard at its nest.*

Glossary

Aerie The nest of an eagle, falcon or hawk, built on a high place.

Breeding season The time of year when male and female animals come together to court and to mate.

Carrion The flesh of a dead animal.

Clutch A set of eggs.

Coniferous Bearing cones; conifers, such as pines and firs, bear cones, stay green all year, and often have needle-shaped leaves.

Conservation The protection and preservation of animals and the countryside in which they live.

Cosmopolitan Belonging to most parts of the world.

Courting display The way in which female and male animals behave before mating occurs.

Deciduous Shedding leaves or loosing foliage at the end of a growing season.

Extinct Having died out completely — an animal or plant which no longer exists.

Food chain The natural cycle of eating and being eaten, for example, a worm may be eaten by a small bird that is itself eaten by a bird of prey.

Habitat The natural home of a plant or animal.

Mating The way in which male and female animals come together so that males can fertilize the females' eggs.

Nomadic Wandering from place to place.

Ornithologist A person who studies birds.

Plague Unusually high numbers of a particular animal or a serious outbreak of a disease.

Predator An animal that hunts and kills another animal for food.

Prey An animal that is hunted and killed by another animal for food.

Scavenge To look for food among garbage.

Taloned Having sharp, hooked claws or talons.

Termite An ant-like insect, which can fly, found mainly in tropical areas.

Tundra The treeless Arctic region where the soil just below ground level is frozen throughout the year.

Finding Out More

If you would like to find out more about birds of prey you might read the following books:

Arnold, Caroline. *Saving the Peregrine Falcon.* Minneapolis, MN: Carolrhoda Books, 1984.

Hogner, Dorothy C. *Birds of Prey.* New York: Harper & Row, 1969.

Hunt, Patricia. *Snowy Owls.* New York: Dodd, Mead, 1982.

McConoughy, Jana. *Bald Eagle.* Mankato, MN: Crestwood House, 1983.

Patent, Dorothy. *Where the Bald Eagles Gather.* Boston: Houghton Mifflin, 1984.

Sadoway, Margaret W. *Owls: Hunters of the Night.* Minneapolis, MN: Lerner Publications, 1981.

Stone, Lynne M. *Birds of Prey.* Chicago, IL: Childrens Press, 1983.

Zim, Herbert. *Owls,* rev. ed. New York: William Morrow, 1977.

Index

Picture Acknowledgements

Bruce Coleman: Roger Wilmshurst cover, Gunter Zieslev 11 (top); Edgar T. Jones 8, 10, 11 (bottom), 15, 16, 26, 27, 28, 29, 32, 35, 40; Gary R. Jones 22; C. Linfoot 37, 38; W. S. Paton/Aquila 20; R. J. Raines 14 (right), 17, 34; Eric Soothill 12, 14 (left), 18 (right), 21, 23, 39, 41 (right), 43 (top); M. J. Thomas opp. title page, 9, 18 (left), 30, 31, 41 (left), 42, 43 (bottom). Artwork by Wendy Meadway.